DANCE *with* Jesus

"Susan has personally experienced one of the deepest forms of grief. Yet she writes this treasure of a book from her point of grace not grief. I plan to give this book to any of my friends that find themselves crying and needing someone who deeply understands."

—**Lysa TerKeurst**, NY Times Best Selling
Author of **The Best Yes**

"THIS is the work of an amazing mom and a stellar woman — a true friend — a mentor — a leader — everything all of us would wish to be. This is her legacy work for her son, and the inspiring journey she took when he left this life. I love someone who stands for such great things and creates inspiration at every turn. Get ready for one of the most inspirational authors of our time and her first of many great works."

—**Mary Agnes Antonopoulos**, Kick-A** Writer,
Social Strategist & Branding Expert

"Several years ago a warm guardian angel named Susan Mead entered my life. You see, as a female football player, I needed a sponsor, so she lovingly adopted me. With her bright eyes, warm embrace, and charming stories, Susan quickly became a delightful combination of sponsor, momma, and friend. Though it was years ago, I will never forget the day Susan looked at me with tears in her heavenly blue eyes and said, "You wouldn't have liked me if you'd met me a few years ago." Then I listened as she told me about losing Kyle, and how

Jesus taught him how to dance. It both broke and warmed my heart to learn how she returned to living and loving after losing her son. I am thrilled that Susan Mead has captured these stories with her genuine warmth and passionate faith; in a way that they resonate to the core of one's being to lift the spirit as you read this book. *Dance With Jesus: From Grief to Grace* is a divine recipe to feed anyone hungering for hope. It is a beautiful story that shares tender morsels of goodness to help heal the soul one page at a time. I encourage you to take up this book, and remember how to dance."

—**Dr. Jen Welter**. BS Business,
MS Sport Psychology, PhD Psychology

"You don't want to miss this book! I had the honor of being at the first reading and I wept like a baby! It brought a deeper measure of healing to a loss of my own. Cannot wait to get my own copy! Thank you Susan."

—**Leslie Brown Baker**

"As you read *Dance With Jesus* your heart will be touched & challenged to cherish the times you have with loved ones & the blessings you have in life. Susan Mead helps capture & direct our priorities with her stories & thought provoking questions. This book shows us how God enables us to dance & live in victory even when faced with such grief."

—**Tim Hancock**, Coaches Director,
Fellowship of Christian Athletes.

As human beings, it's difficult to understand why bad things happen to good people. As Susan shares their story, we are reminded that the Holy Spirit comes to comfort us, Abba Father longs to wrap His loving arms around us and Jesus Christ waits to dance – if we only take His hands.

—**Richard Wright**, CEO & President, AdvoCare International, LLP., Ernst & Young Entrepreneur Of The Year Award Winner — 2013

Thou hast turned for me
my mourning into dancing:
thou hast put off my sackcloth,
and girded me with gladness…
Psalm 30:11

DANCE
with Jesus

FROM GRIEF TO *Grace*

SUSAN B. MEAD

NEW YORK

DANCE *with* Jesus
FROM GRIEF TO *Grace*

Published in New York, New York, by Morgan James Publishing. Morgan James and The Entrepreneurial Publisher are trademarks of Morgan James, LLC.
www.MorganJamesPublishing.com

The Morgan James Speakers Group can bring authors to your live event. For more information or to book an event visit The Morgan James Speakers Group at www.TheMorganJamesSpeakersGroup.com.

Scripture marked NIV is taken from the Holy Bible, New International Version®, NIV®. Copyright © 1973, 1978, 1984, 2011 by Biblica Inc.™ Used by permission of Zondervan. All rights reserved worldwide (www.zondervan.com). The "NIV" and "New International Version" are trademarks registered in the United States Patent and Trademark Office by Biblica Inc.™ Scripture marked KJV is taken from the King James Version of the Holy Bible.

A **free** eBook edition is available with the purchase of this print book.

CLEARLY PRINT YOUR NAME ABOVE IN UPPER CASE

Instructions to claim your free eBook edition:
1. Download the BitLit app for Android or iOS
2. Write your name in **UPPER CASE** on the line
3. Use the BitLit app to submit a photo
4. Download your eBook to any device

ISBN 978-1-63047-307-5 paperback
ISBN 978-1-63047-308-2 eBook
ISBN 978-1-63047-309-9 hardcover
ISBN 978-1-63047-439-3 audio
Library of Congress Control Number:
2014942211

Cover Design by:
Rachel Lopez
www.r2cdesign.com

Interior Design by:
Bonnie Bushman
bonnie@caboodlegraphics.com

In an effort to support local communities, raise awareness and funds, Morgan James Publishing donates a percentage of all book sales for the life of each book to Habitat for Humanity Peninsula and Greater Williamsburg.

236

Get involved today, visit
www.MorganJamesBuilds.com.

Habitat for Humanity®
Peninsula and
Greater Williamsburg
Building Partner

39300005590145

Would you like to Dance with Jesus? Please visit here to join the dance:

www.DanceWithJesus.com

Have you ever thought that you have no space or time in your life for the people who matter most to you? Create space for them. It may be the last kind word, hug, or kiss you get to share with them. You deserve that special, sacred time too.

Things get broken, discarded, or replaced. *People matter.*

TABLE OF CONTENTS

How to Use This Book

Dance With Jesus: From Grief to Grace was written for a person experiencing grief. It is a quick read for the grief-stricken individual, as grief can shorten the attention span.

Grief touches us all, whether we're a parent or grandparent who has lost a child/grandchild, a sibling who has lost a brother or sister, a son or daughter who has lost a parent, or anyone who has had to face loss due to terminal disease or tragic accident within their family or circle of friends. When the tragedy of death strikes, we need to KNOW that GOD is still alive and restoring His fragile, broken sons and daughters today.

In my darkest moment and deepest despair, I turned to the story of OTHERS who had walked a similar path.

And saw HOPE.

If they could, surely I could . . .

We are wired to seek God—the One True God—and we want to know He is alive, moving, and making a difference in our—His precious children's—lives. Yes, even today. He is with us, always and forevermore. When we seek Him, God reveals Himself to calm the raging storms of our lives.

My desire is that *Dance With Jesus: From Grief to Grace* will help people think differently about how God *can* and *does* act in their lives by illustrating ways He has shown up in the life of one of His broken, bereaved daughters. Only God can pierce the darkness of our heart and mind, creating a deeper awareness of and craving for a more intimate, personal relationship with Him that restores our soul.

Spoken from the perspective of a life-long Christian, this story reveals the ups and downs—and out-of-control spirals—of life. The chapters open with a relevant Scripture verse, followed by an account of an up-close and personal experience with God. Each chapter concludes with thought-provoking questions designed for personal use as the spotlight is turned from me onto YOU, the reader.

So you can reflect on God
> and how He is showing up in YOUR life
> > to heal YOUR brokenness.

Psalm 147:3 says, "He heals the brokenhearted and binds up their wounds."

May you see, and feel, His Mighty hand at work in your life, healing, binding your wounds and loving YOU.

Would you like to join the dance . . . and dance with Jesus?
www.DanceWithJesus.com

ACKNOWLEDGMENTS

Holt Mead—My soul mate. You lift me up. When we had the boys, I told you I needed you. When we lost Kyle, I told you "I need you, forever." In reality…I love you more deeply day by day. Did I share that I need you…for eternity?

Matt Mead—My delight! You are my gift from God, Matt. Natural leader. Amazing cook. Fun spirit…with blue eyes and a smile that melts my heart. I love you…from the very core of my being.

Mom and Dad—You raised me well, and I love you both dearly. You introduced me to "Our Father," who art in heaven.

My siblings, Chuck and Margaret, and yes, Bette too. And their spouses and children, Amanda and Libby; David, Emma, and Kenneth; Robert (now married to Myriam), Kathryn, and Bobby. I love each one of you.

Richard and Sherry Wright—President, CEO, and Executive VP of AdvoCare. Dear friends first and foremost. You two cared enough to reach through my grief to give me a glimmer of hope.

What did we lose?

- 168 pounds: 5 sizes for me and 12 inches off of Holt's waist
- $150,000 debt, paid off

What did we gain?

- Energy to live and play!
- With the excess weight gone, we regained our health
- Debt freedom
- The choice to retire from corporate America— ten years *early*
- Time freedom

You two put some sunshine back into my life…and money in my pocket! You helped me compress time to gain time freedom. People matter. How much is it worth to have time to help a friend, become a friend, or be a friend? A deep and abiding thank you.

Would you like to see Holt's story? Check it out at www. Fit4Champs.com.

Crystal Thurber—You challenge(d!) me to be better. Every day. Still do. And I love you, my precious friend.

Bob Beaudine—You did not know me, yet you took time to pour wisdom into me, Bob. You inspire me to look for the divine appointments that our great God inserts into each day. The power of WHO. You've got the greatest WHO! Thank you, Bob.

Amanda Rooker—You took the time to read the manuscript. And gave me hope that these words are intended for a bigger audience than just me. And your Split-Seed team is stellar! Thank you.

Derrill Hagood—You made these words come alive and dance on the pages. Thank you.

Terry Whalin—Thank you for introducing me to Amanda Rooker, and for requesting the manuscript upon hearing her words. I am honored, truly honored, to know you.

Morgan James Publishing—Thank you, the entire team, for your diligence in bringing this book to life. May this be the first of many.

Mary Agnes & Tommy Antonopoulos—How do I say thank you? Your work is impeccable. Thank you for making space to add me into your busy, busy life, as a client, and more importantly, as a cherished friend.

Dr. Jen Welter—My friend. You may have read about her—the first woman to play professional football with the men in a non-kicking position. She played for the Texas Revolution, an Indoor Football League (IFL) team. She's five-foot-two. Yep, she can run through me. Probably through you too! Jen literally held my hand when she started training me. What a heart she has to help others be the best they can be.

My Coppell Women's Club friends—Cherished friends. You encourage me. And I treasure each one of you.

Bethel Dallas—My church family. Thank you, each one of you. You hold my heart in your hands...and lift me up.

Danny and Diane McDaniel—Thank you for walking with me into a deeper relationship with God. There are no adequate words to describe the depth of emotion and degree of thankfulness I have for the two of you. New eyes. New heart. New life.

James and Betty Robison—Thank you for your devotion to God. Faithful service for over fifty years. He delights in you. Both of you. And Jesus is dancing with your precious Robin. Just like you saw her so many years ago, Betty. I pray that brings you great joy.

Water for LIFE—Mommas are burying their babies around the world—simply due to lack of, or contaminated, water. That is *not ok*. We CAN make a difference. Ten percent of the proceeds from the sale of this book, *Dance with Jesus: From Grief to Grace*, will benefit Water for LIFE to help dig water wells in remote, forgotten places for remote, forgotten people. We remember. And choose to reach out a helping hand.

So I thank you, the readers of this book. You are making a difference in a life—for a child of God somewhere in this precious world. From my heart to yours, my deepest, most sincere thank you.

Would you like to know more about Water for LIFE? If so, please visit here: http://www.ambassadorsforlife.org/dancewithjesus

Dear heavenly Father, from the pen in my hand to Your compassionate, loving heart, may these words honor You. Touch the hearts, souls, and spirits of Your precious children. Reveal Yourself, Lord, and order our steps…

Upon reading this book, you may be compelled to answer the questions in each chapter. Please do! The best story has yet to be told…it's yours.

You are cordially invited to join the dance…
www.DanceWithJesus.com

Chapter 1

WHERE IS MATT?

1 Peter 3:13-15 (NIV)

Who is going to harm you if you are eager to do good? But even if you should suffer for what is right, you are blessed. "Do not fear what they fear; do not be frightened." But in your hearts revere Christ as Lord. Always be prepared to give an answer to everyone who asks you to give the reason for the hope that you have. But do this with gentleness and respect...

1

Lafayette, Louisiana.

That's the answer to "Where is Matt?" He's my oldest son. Next time you are in Lafayette, Louisiana, go eat at 2Paul's Radically Urban Barbeque on Johnston in the Albertson's shopping center. It's near the University of Louisiana Lafayette (ULL). Or head to their second location in Broussard, just south of Lafayette. Tell the blue-eyed guy in the kitchen, "Hey, your momma said to get the pulled pork salad." You'll be glad you did!

Dancing with Jesus.

That's the answer to the next question, "Where is Kyle?" He's my youngest son. Now and forever twenty.

I'm so blessed.

Did you expect that to be the next sentence? No? Yes!

Let me share why I can say that I'm blessed—and mean it from the very bottom of my heart.

Personal Reflection

First, let me ask you a question—do you know that you are blessed?

Chapter 2

GOD GETS HIS MONEY

Psalm 25:6-10 (NIV)

Remember, LORD, your great mercy and love, for they are from of old. Remember not the sins of my youth and my rebellious ways; according to your love remember me, for you, Lord, are good. Good and upright is the LORD; therefore he instructs sinners in his ways. He guides the humble in what is right and teaches them his way. All the ways of the LORD are loving and faithful toward those who keep the demands of his covenant.

I've known Jesus Christ my entire life.

My cousin Susan came down from Northern Virginia to Texas to be my godmother when I was baptized as an infant in the Episcopal Church of the Good Shepherd in Terrell, Texas. I heard stories about how Susan asked "What did they put in the dirt to make it so black?" every time we drove from home in Wills Point, Texas, to Dallas. We loved our trips there, whether it was to shop, go to a movie or pick up a friend from the airport, it was ALWAYS a fun outing. Susan was familiar with red clay and we were blessed to live where the sandy East Texas soil met the edge of the black dirt belt that runs through North Central Texas. That soil simply looks rich to me!

We were in that church every Sunday for church services and Wednesday for choir practice with my parents. When I was about three or four years old, I heard something one Sunday that got my little mind *busy*. The offering was blessed and what I recall hearing was, "This is God's money to use as He wills."

So what was my young mind busy with? How does God get His money? Literally. HOW? They said He uses it, so He had to get it. Right? Doesn't that make sense—when you are three or four?

I thought about it for days. And days. (That's forever when you are that age!) We did all kinds of typical errands with Mom that week: grocery store, post office to mail a package, drug store, airport to take Daddy somewhere. Just a regular week.

And then, during the service the following Sunday morning, sitting on the front row (yes indeed, that's where Daddy lined up his crew each week), they blessed the offering to God's use once again—and I got it! I *saw* how God got His money.

God's money
    To use as He wills
        Post office
            Brown paper wrapping
        AIR MAIL STAMP
    BIG JET

Here's what I saw:

Father Flagg wrapped up God's money—oh, so carefully.

Wrapped THAT package in plain brown paper wrapping (disguised—so cleverly disguised, I thought).

Addressed that package:

GOD

HEAVEN

    STAMPED that wrapping paper with AIR MAIL

       And flew it—in a BIG JET

    Up as close to heaven as possible

And threw it out

For God to reach down from heaven with His powerful hands to GET HIS MONEY.

To use as He wills.

Tada! There I sat with arms crossed and a satisfied nod as I figured out *that* puzzle. Can't you just see that smug little grin? I still laugh when I recall how absolutely sure and totally satisfied I felt when I figured that one out.

I got to sing in the choir with the adults from the time I was about seven years old. Would you like to know that I need a bucket to carry a tune? Sure do! There were a few folks I remember from my childhood time at this lovely old church. Harry Madgwick sang in the choir and he was simply regal to me! Strong British name, beautiful voice, and quite the handsome gentleman to this little girl from East Texas. Another member I recall was May—a beautiful British lady. Her son drove a Jaguar—in Texas—in the early 1960s. *Wow*! Big stretch Jaguar—like the car the Big Bad Wolf drove in Little Red Riding Hood cartoons. LONG hood. Seemed to literally stretch into space as he drove around a corner. COOL CAR. Very cool. You know what? That car may have been one of a handful of Jaguar's in all of Texas at that time—I was smitten!

When I was confirmed, the bishop who confirmed me had his mitered hat on and I promise you he must have been the proverbial "ten feet tall." At least that's what he looked like to this twelve-year-old kid! I have such fond memories of the wonderful people in that lovely old church, the beautiful stained glass, and the historic pipe organ. And God's money. And that cool car.

As a child, my mom taught me that I was never alone as Jesus is love and is always with us. She even said, "Hold His hand when you pray. He will hold your hand too. And you will feel His presence and power." Oh, yes! When I pray—to this very day—my hands are typically clasped—and I feel Him, squeezing my hand back! Jesus' power and presence is real, tangible, and comforting.

Imagine:
You are fifteen years old.
Remember how you felt as a teenager?
Oh, but Jesus was there, whenever I prayed.

COMFORT

JOY

PEACE

Holding my hand.

Didn't get me to be perfect—but that's a different story!

His presence got me through every day. How blessed is that?

Personal Reflection

- Remember your teen years—were they filled with rebellion or reverence?
- Have you ever held the hand of God, or felt his presence with you? Would you like to feel God's presence in your life?

Chapter 3

CAN'T SHOOT 'TIL NOON

Psalm 139:13-16 (NIV)

For you created my inmost being;
You knit me together in my mother's womb.
I praise you because I am fearfully and wonderfully made:
Your works are wonderful,
I know that full well.
My frame was not hidden from you
when I was made in the secret place.
When I was woven together in the depths of the earth,

13

your eyes saw my unformed body.
All the days ordained for me
Were written in your book
Before one of them came to be.

I met the love of my life at college in Monroe, Louisiana. It was called Northeast Louisiana University then. Now it's the University of Louisiana Monroe.

Holt Mead simply stole my heart at nineteen. We married at the ripe old age of twenty-two—and thought we were so grown up! Holt's dad was a retired Methodist minister in the Louisiana Conference, so he performed the wedding ceremony.

We married. At one o'clock on Saturday afternoon, September 1, 1979. Holt wanted his parents home safe and sound before dark. Remember, *retired* minister.

My dad simply said, "Can't shoot 'til noon."

You see, September first is opening day for dove season. Dad and I had a tradition of going dove hunting on opening day—until September 1, 1979! Do you think my dad would have liked an evening wedding?!

We joke that we had about one hundred ladies and ten gentlemen (the ones in the ceremony mostly!) at the service. Dad said all the other guys were out huntin'…

Five and a half years later, we were blessed with Matthew Alexander Mead. His name means "gift from God, defender of man." He truly is my gift! He looks just like me and acts just like Holt. Great combination, if I do say so myself.

When Matt was born, he cried loudly, like babies do as they are cleaned up. The nurse handed Matt to Holt. Matt quit crying. Hmmm. The nurse took Matt back—he cried. She handed Matt to me—and he quit crying. He knew us! Praise God, Matt knew us! He totally wrapped himself around my heart at that moment. I had been in love with Matt ever since I learned we were expecting him. And I always will be. Even when boys will be boys…

Two years and five months later, we were blessed with Kyle Wilson Mead. We found out we were expecting him three days after I gave away all my maternity clothes and were in the midst of a move from Dallas to Tampa, Florida.

We were at my parents' house in North Louisiana and by then I suspected I might be pregnant. My sister, Margaret, and I are both medical technologists, and she was headed to work on Christmas Eve, where she would be able to perform the test for me—if we could get a blood sample for her to take to work with her. We scrambled around the house until we found one of Dad's 1 mL allergy shot syringes—which she used to draw my blood for a pregnancy test. This was way before the days of heading to the grocery store or pharmacy for your own kit. She called early the next morning saying, "Merry Christmas."

When Kyle was born, he looked just like Holt. I fell head over heels in love with that little guy, right then and there. And Matt adored his little brother. Soft hands. Matt had such soft hands with Kyle—'til they were older and wrestlin'.

Life took us from Tampa, to North Carolina, to Dallas, up to New Jersey, south to Shreveport, Louisiana, and then back to the Dallas area.

Holt told me when we got married that he never wanted to move again as he had moved too many times growing up as a preacher's kid. I have a question.

Are we done moving yet?

Personal Reflection

- 🕊 Do you have any children or godchildren?
- 🕊 Were you present for the birth of your child, niece or nephew, or godchild?
- 🕊 What about when you found out you were pregnant—were there any memorable moments?
- 🕊 What is memorable about the birth of your first child, niece, nephew, or godchild? What was heartwarming? Blessed? Beautiful?
- 🕊 If you had any subsequent children, what was memorable about their births?
- 🕊 What warms your heart to share with them and others about the day?
- 🕊 What makes you smile when you recall it? Does it bring tears of joy to your eyes?

Chapter 4

JOANIE'S IN THAT BOX

1 John 4:4 (NIV)

You are of God, little children, and have overcome them,
because He who is in you is greater than he who is in the world.

While we were living in Shreveport, we had most of the family over one sunny summer weekend. Oh, what a game of canasta we played! I bet it was one for the record books. My sister Bette

19

had a hand the likes of which none of us had ever seen—before or since. Her score was 5,700 points—for a single hand!

Bette's six-year-old daughter Kathryn was also there with us. She was very intrigued by a beautiful carved box on my mantle. You see, Joanie was in that box.

Huh? Who was Joanie?

Joanie was Kyle's black lab. Jersey Joan Jett. Joanie.

Joanie died of cancer earlier that year, when she was only about five years old. We had not figured out where to bury a big black lab in the muddy red clay of Shreveport, Louisiana, so we had her cremated, and her ashes were in that lovely carved box. We still had not decided where to bury her ashes, so the gorgeous box was on the mantle in the hearth room.

Kathryn simply wanted to open the box—to see Joanie!

Can you just imagine it? What a mess it would be if the box was pried open—dust and ashes all over everywhere, instead of a bubbly black lab to lick that cute six-year-old girl. It took some convincing to keep that box up high on the mantle and sealed!

Personal Reflection

- Out of the mouths of babes comes such delight! What have you heard from a little one that you will remember forever?
- Who said it, how old were they, and why did it strike a chord with you?
- Did it make you laugh—or cry—or laugh so hard you cried?

Chapter 5

SHE'S MINE

Psalm 109:26-27 (NIV)
Help me, O LORD my God;
save me in accordance with your love.
Let them know that it is your hand,
that you, O Lord, have done it.

The following month, Mom called on a Tuesday morning. Early.

23

It had been an odd day for me on Monday, the afternoon before. I had a migraine headache that sent me to bed for a couple of hours. That was unusual for me. I rarely got headaches. *Rarely.*

Mom asked, "Did Holt tell you that I called last night?" No. It was not unusual, as we sometimes forgot to share when folks called. She had simply asked him to have me call her back. I thought nothing of it.

Until Mom said, "Bette killed herself. Yesterday afternoon."

Oh, God.

How?

She bought a gun…

My precious middle sister, Bette, was dead. She was a brilliant PhD nurse, and everyone at her hospital called her sunshine. Oh, God!

And it had happened while I was suffering from a rare, debilitating migraine. Empathy? She was two inches shorter than me, but she looked and sounded just like me when we talked.

Then I felt it. "It" can only be described as an angel wing… or the hand of God.

It stroked my heart. (I felt Your hand stroke my broken heart, Lord.)

And I heard—out loud—"I've got her. She's mine." Possessive—*mine*.

The peace that passes all understanding enveloped me. I went from believing to knowing that God not only had, but still has, Bette wrapped in His loving arms.

He told me so. And I believe God. Then chaos ensued.

Personal Reflection

- 🕉 Have you felt God's hand in your life?
- 🕉 Have you heard Him speak to you?
- 🕉 Have you heard Him speak out loud to you?
- 🕉 Have you moved from believing in God to knowing that God is real?

Chapter 6

Big Old Ugly Hairy Spider

Psalm 103:13-17 (NIV)

As a father has compassion on his children,
so the LORD has compassion on those who fear him;
for he knows how we are formed,
he remembers that we are dust.
As for man, his days are like grass,
he flourishes like a flower of the field;
the wind blows over it and it is gone,
and its place remembers it no more.

27

But from everlasting to everlasting
the LORD'S love is with those who fear him.
And his righteousness with their children's children...

Robert, Bette's husband, wanted to bury her next to his dad up in their family cemetery in St. Joe, Arkansas. Bette called this area near the Buffalo River "God's country." Robert's dad was a surgeon who loved Bette dearly and treasured the nursing skills that she lavished upon him. She loved being able to nurse him in his later life and final days. We all thought that that was the perfect place for Bette to be laid to rest.

Kathryn, my niece, and Bobby, my nephew, were helping me plant daffodil bulbs in their mom's grave after the service was over, folks had left and the dirt was being placed back into the grave. We were pitching bulbs in one by one, when, to our surprise, a huge tarantula crawled out of the dirt pile next to us. We flung all the rest of the bulbs into the grave with one big heave, and off we flew! At that point, we (or more accurately, I) did not care where they landed.

The kids burst out laughing at the antics of their hysterical aunt, as I scrambled away from that big old ugly hairy spider!

God certainly has a sense of humor—what a memory to seal that day.

The following Christmas, six-year-old Kathryn asked me if I had her mom in a box like Joanie. We all hooted with laughter and reminded her, "Oh no honey, we buried your mom— remember the spider?"

Oh yeah. That's right!

Bless those precious children, Lord, as they grow into young adulthood. May you continue to find favor in them, their dad, Robert, and his beautiful new bride, Myriam, whom we love.

Personal Reflection

- Have you ever had a moment of pure hilarity on an otherwise somber day?
- Did the humor brighten everyone's heavy spirits?
- Does it make you smile when you recall or share that precious, sacred moment?
- Did you feel like God wanted you to experience His joy?

Chapter 7

TATTOO TABOO

Leviticus 19:28 (NIV)
*Do not cut your bodies for the dead or put
tattoo marks on yourselves. I am the LORD.*

James 4:12 (NIV)
*There is only one Lawgiver and Judge,
the one who is able to save and destroy.*

Financial support ceases.

That was the rule about a tattoo showing up on one of our boy's bodies—until the day that Kyle walked in with a huge tattoo covering his arm from shoulder to elbow.

Only God can judge me

Yep, superimposed on a cross, sunbeams, and clouds.

Hmmm. Okay, God. Your name is carved on Kyle's arm. Your name is proudly sported for the world to see Kyle's belief in You.

Financial support ceases with a tattoo. That's the rule. Right?

It seems we reevaluated our stance on the "tattoo taboo," as God's name was etched on our son's arm—even in light of the scripture prohibiting tattoos.

Did I mention that we are very much a work in progress, in walking closer with God—and obeying Him and His Word?

Personal Reflection

- Do you have a tattoo or know someone who does?
- Does it honor someone or something?
- Is there meaning or significance in the tattoo?

Chapter 8

LIVING TO DIE AT HOME

Ecclesiastes 7:1-4 (NIV)
A good name is better than fine perfume,
and the day of death better than the day of birth.
It is better to go to a house of mourning
than to go to a house of feasting,
for death is the destiny of every man;
the living should take this to heart.
Sorrow is better than laughter,
because a sad face is good for the heart.

The heart of the wise is in the house of mourning,
but the heart of fools is in the house of pleasure.

Aunt Wrenette was my husband's sister. She was ten years older than Holt, and she graduated from Louisiana State University with her master's degree in library science. Wrenette was a very beautiful, tall, slender, reserved woman with the most striking silver hair. She was never blessed with children, but I tell you what—she sure loved good wine, good cooking, a good book, and her husband Allen—and her two nephews, Matt and Kyle! I always admired her ability to get full from just a few bites of food. She savored, absolutely savored, every morsel. Is there a lesson in that for us?

She met the love of her life, Allen Whartenby, at LSU. He was working on his master's degree in library science, even though he already had a PhD.

Allen was a student of history, a deep thinker, yet fun to know. He was a small man in stature, with a *massive* intellect. He had his pilot's license. He had taught French at prestigious universities in the US and in France; he loved Italy, good books, good wine, and Wrenette. Did I mention that he could cook? You wanted to be invited over for dinner—I promise!

Wrenette was about eighteen years younger than Allen, so my brother-in-law was about five years younger than my parents. He battled cancer—a couple of different kinds of cancer. Oh, how he fought!

Allen was in the hospital over Easter weekend. He was living to get home—to die. Allen was adamant that he did not want to die in the hospital. He wanted to be home with Wrenette. He was a private man who wanted to share that moment with his precious wife.

Hospice was finally ready for Allen in the late afternoon, the day after Easter. Kyle lifted Uncle Allen out of the hospital bed, into the wheelchair, rolled him out through the hospital to their car, lifted Uncle Allen out of the wheelchair into the car, followed them home, lifted Uncle Allen out of the car, carried him into the house, and placed Uncle Allen into the hospice bed—from which Uncle Allen passed away the following morning.

Allen did not want a funeral, just a memorial service. Wrenette scheduled it for Friday, which was Kyle's last day of spring break.

The last place we saw Kyle alive was at his Uncle Allen's memorial service.

Aunt Wrenette was devastated, absolutely devastated, by the double whammy of losses:

Losing Allen, the love of her life, on Tuesday.
Holding a memorial service for Allen on Friday.
Losing her youngest nephew, Kyle, on Saturday.
Burying Kyle the following week.
All so close together.
She grieved. *Deeply.*

Personal Reflection

- Have you ever felt a double whammy of grief? Or a triple whammy?
- Have you ever been completely overwhelmed?
- Does reading this take your breath away right now, because you are in the midst of grief yourself?

Chapter 9

BROKEN TO BREATHING

Colossians 3:13 (NIV)

*Bear with each other and forgive one another if any of you has
a grievance against someone. Forgive as the Lord forgave you.*

We had the pallbearers lined up for Kyle's service. Both hockey
teams that Kyle had played for were going to be honor guards,
and his closest friends were the pallbearers. One of his dearest

friends, Steven Robertson, whom we call Bub, even flew into Louisiana from Sydney, Australia, to serve as a pallbearer for Kyle. And a friend on the Isle of Wight lit a candle for this twenty-year-old young man. How is it that some folks know people all over the world? Even in a short twenty years, Kyle *lived*—exuberantly!

Imagine my horror, then, when I found out that one of Kyle's closest friends, Kenny, had been with Kyle when he purchased drugs which, combined with a beer later that evening, caused respiratory distress, resulting in Kyle's death. Kyle's body was still in Lafayette and the funeral was to be scheduled once he had been released from the morgue and transported up to Shreveport, so timing was still up in the air at that point.

I immediately called Matt to say that I could *not* have Kenny as a pallbearer. Matt's words were simple, eloquent, and have subsequently changed the course of my life: "Mom, God's already forgiven Kenny. You need to too."

"Oh, Matthew, I will have to pray about that." And the burden lifted a little. God gave me the grace to forgive Kenny, for Kenny had—and still has—the heaviest load to bear. He carries it each and every day. His friend died. That cannot be changed. **However, it is our response to an event that shows our character, not the event itself.** So how was I going to respond?

I called Kenny the next day to let him know how absolutely disappointed I was in the decision that they both made, but Kyle loved him and would want Kenny there for him—and I would be honored for him to be a pallbearer for Kyle. Kenny is doing well to this very day—and served our country with honor. *Rejoice!*

And that's God—pouring His grace out on His children. You see, God knew we both needed His grace—to move from broken to breathing to blessed, free, and forgiven.

Personal Reflection

- ᔈ Have you needed to forgive someone? Did you forgive them?
- ᔈ Have you prayed to God to lift that burden off of you—and then freely given the load to Him?
- ᔈ Did you feel the burden lighten?

Chapter 10

I Taught Him How ...
To Dance

Psalm 30:11 (KJV)

Thou hast turned for me my mourning into dancing:
thou hast put off my sackcloth, and girded me with gladness...

When we lost Kyle, his dear friends prepared a banner of photos from the time he had been in Lafayette, Louisiana, playing hockey (yep—ice hockey in South Louisiana!). He played for both the Cajun Catahoulas and the University of Louisiana Lafayette Ragin' Cajuns. These were priceless moments captured and shared:

- Kyle and Meredith, his girlfriend, dripping wet and kissing in the rain at a parade.
- Matt and Kyle at the Saint Paddy's Day parade in NOLA (that's Louisiana speak for New Orleans).
- Awesome (pronounced with an Australian emphasis!) friends, Bub, Kyle, and Charlene in the shower...oh, yes, fully clothed. Why? It was Charlene's birthday and they were having a BLAST! Did I share that when Kyle showed up—anywhere—a party usually broke out? Oh, yes. He was FUN to know!
- Three guys: Jordan, Bud—not Bub from Australia—Bud, and Kyle, having a toga party. At Jordan's house. Just them, just because. If there was ever an opportunity to dress up, in ANY costume, Kyle would champion that endeavor! You know. PARTY TIME!
- Kyle dancing at the ice rink, wearing his favorite Scooby Doo tee shirt, blazer, and jeans. He is about eight inches from the floor. He could get down—way down!

On the morning of Kyle's service, I had a dream.

Kyle was dancing—like the photo—with *Jesus*! This was the day before I saw the banner with the photo...

Jesus turned, looked at me, and said, "This is to bring you great joy. I taught him how. I taught him how to dance."

Can you imagine? Jesus was clad in a white robe with a beige overlay, which was the same color as Kyle's blazer, with a royal purple sash from shoulder to waist, and He was way down—right there with Kyle!

Thank You, and praise Your holy name, Jesus.

So, where's Kyle?

How would you answer that question?

I believe he's dancing with Jesus.

Personal Reflection

- Have you lost someone precious to you?
- Or are you in the process of losing someone dear to you now?
- Have you had a moment when God revealed Himself to you, or showed you your precious someone?
- Were they in heaven or somewhere else?
- Did this help you understand that they were okay, so that you could move forward?

Chapter 11

HE'S IN MY PRESENCE

Psalm 17:15 (NIV)
And I—in righteousness I will see your face;
when I awake, I will be satisfied with seeing your likeness.

Revelation 7:13 (NIV)
Then one of the elders asked me, "These in white robes—
who are they, and where did they come from?"

Two days later, God gave me the gift of another dream. Don't you just love unwrapping His gifts? I treasure each and every gift from God. It's like He extravagantly pours His love out upon us, His precious children! And we get to savor every single moment.

Kyle's hands and face were his hands and face, but he was clad in:

White light

Ethereal, heavenly garb

(How do you describe heavenly things?)

The background was a rich chocolate brown tone.

I had not read the book of Revelation at that time, so I did not know about white clothes in heaven. And why was the background brown—heaven is supposed to be light, right?

Kyle was flat on his tummy, like a baby, with his knees tucked up under his belly and his feet under his rear (like a folded pose) with his arms *stretched* out, as far as they could go, before the face of God.

"He's in My presence, in absolute adulation and supplication; he's in My presence," said God.

Thank You, Lord God Almighty. Praise Your holy name!

The Lord knew what this grieving mom needed:

To get out of bed…
 That day…
  And the next…
   And the next…
    And the next…

Personal Reflection

- 🐍 Has God revealed something significant to you?
- 🐍 Did it help you through a difficult moment?
- 🐍 Did it help you get out of bed the next morning, knowing you could face that day?
- 🐍 Is there a new purpose for your life?
- 🐍 Do you feel blessed? Restored?

Chapter 12

THE DARK AND BROKEN PLACES

Job 3:4-5 (NIV)
[Job Speaks]
That day—may it turn to darkness;
may God above not care about it;
may no light shine on it.
May gloom and utter darkness claim it once more;
may a cloud settle over it;
may blackness overwhelm it.

Lamentations 3:1-6 (NIV)

I am the man who has seen affliction
by the rod of the Lord's wrath.
He has driven me away and made me walk
in darkness rather than light;
indeed, he has turned his hand against me
again and again, all day long.
He has made my skin and my flesh grow old
and has broken my bones.
He has besieged me and surrounded me
with bitterness and hardship.
He has made me dwell in darkness
like those long dead.

Darkness
> Gloom
>> Cloud covered
>>> Blackness
>>>> Affliction
>>>>> Wrath
>>>>>> Driving me away
>>>>> Walk in darkness
>>>> Broken
>>> Besieged
>> Bitterness
> Hardship

Darkness

Ring a bell? It all felt like an arrow that pierced my heart. The words even look like one too! **The dark and broken places...**

The words sound like the broken places I lived in during the early days without Kyle. Black. My world turned black: tasted black, felt black, looked black, was black.

Abandoned.
  Alone.
    Sad.
      Useless.
        Pointless.
          Rudderless.
            Numb.
              Lost.
                Black.

I did not know how to cope, manage, think, or communicate. Or live. Did I even want to? It seems like a common thought for parents who have lost a child.

WHY? Followed by *why bother*? Even with a husband, son, and family to love, and people who needed me, I still felt lost. I was incapable of helping them heal, when I was so broken myself. They felt lost too. No one knew how to communicate his or her needs during this painful, heartbreaking time of utter loss. None of us. We just stumbled through the days. And awoke too many nights gasping for breath.

Matt was living in South Louisiana, three hours away. I texted Matt and said, "I need to know you are okay—every day"—kind of like a mom of a three-year-old versus a twenty-three-year-old. I think he needed to know we were okay too.

Hearing from Matt each day allowed me to breathe. And on the days his cell phone died, I thought I would drive to South Louisiana myself—just to see him alive and breathing!

Personal Reflection

- 🍥 Are you experiencing similar feelings of great loss right now?
- 🍥 Have you looked for a friend to guide you, who has walked the path you are on?
- 🍥 Have you read any books that let you know you are not alone?
- 🍥 Are you seeking counsel from a trusted source?
- 🍥 If your world is too black, please call for help. Now. It's available!
- 🍥 In the United States, call 1-800-273-8255 for the National Suicide Prevention Lifeline.
  OR
  For a veteran, please use veteranscrisisline.net.
- 🍥 *You matter*. People are available to help you. Right now. Reach out.

Chapter 13

LIVING AND LOVING
AFTER LOSING

John 12:46 (NIV)

*I have come into the world as a light, so that
no one who believes in me should stay in darkness.*

2 Corinthians 4:6 (NIV)

For God, who said, "Let light shine out of darkness," made his light shine in our hearts to give us the light of the knowledge of God's glory displayed in the face of Christ.

I read. And read. And read some more! I read everything I could get my hands on about grief. I simply needed to know that I was not alone. Nor that I was the only one experiencing these feelings—or were they crushing emotions?

Carol Gekakis and Harold Turner showed me that I could live. They both had figured out their "new normal" after losing a son. If they could, I could too. Carol and Harold, I do not know if you realize what anchors you were for me. Thank you.

Hope arises...

Don Piper, in *90 Minutes in Heaven*, describes visiting heaven after a car accident. I lived in that chapter, as it filled me with hope. I also went to hear Mr. Piper speak...twice! Kyle was perfect now. Even though I was far from it...

Seeing others living and loving after losing a child gave me hope that I too could turn a corner and come out of the darkness into a brighter spot.

So did I do that? How did I do that?

Time.

The passage of time has softened the ragged edges of grief. Do I miss Kyle? *Absolutely.* Every day. I want a big old bear hug from him and for him to nuzzle his head into the crook of my neck like he did as a kid. Or—can you believe this—the smell of his nasty hockey bag. I miss that tremendously.

Do I want him back here with me? Yes—for a moment. Then I realize just how selfish that would be, because he is now in Paradise with Jesus. Can you imagine? Celebrating on the streets of gold, wrapped in the glory of God—and being taken away from that?

Don Piper also talks about his return from heaven…and his longing to return to the throne of grace in God's presence.

I had to accept that Kyle is no longer here, regardless of how much I would like him to be. He is in heaven now. Oh, Lord.

And yes, thank You, Lord. You showed me where he is—*hope!*

Personal Reflection

- ❧ Is the hole in your heart so big that you feel like you have collapsed into it?
- ❧ Are you experiencing the raw, ragged edges of grief?
- ❧ Are you looking for a place to turn to—in hopes that a bright spot will appear, if even for a moment?
- ❧ Has a little time elapsed?
- ❧ Have the edges softened? Or are they still ragged?
- ❧ Is there a part of your lost loved one that you long to see, smell, touch, hear, taste?
- ❧ Are you starting to accept your loss?
- ❧ Have you found hope somewhere yet?

Chapter 14

MY HIGHER POWER
IS MESSING WITH ME

Matthew 5:4 (NIV)

Blessed are those who mourn, for they will be comforted.

Matthew grieved. And we prayed for, and over, our oldest son. The women's group at the church also prayed for Matt.

One Sunday afternoon, our group of women prayed that the Lord would touch Matt's heart, comfort him, and let Matt know that God loved him and was there with him.

Matt called me less than an hour later.

"Mom," Matt said, "my higher power is messing with me!"

I burst out laughing.

"What?" He had to know why I was laughing.

"Well, precious," I said, "a group of women just lifted your name to the Lord God in heaven, asking Him to comfort you, and to convict you of His love for you. Of course, He is messing with you!"

Matt continues to walk through some very trying times. He grieved, and grieved, and continues to grieve. Oh, Father God. Hold us both in Your loving hands. Comfort us, both of us—and comfort Holt, my precious husband. Please hold Matt close, Father God. Please heal the depths of his wounded, broken heart—and Holt's as well.

I prayed that God would carve His name in Matt's heart. Our whole women's ministry at the church prayed with me for Matt and Holt.

Personal Reflection

- ☞ Do you have a family member who is grieving?
- ☞ Do you feel ill-equipped to help them?
- ☞ Do you have a group of people to join you in prayer for them?

Chapter 15

CARVE HIS NAME

Proverbs 22:6 (NIV)
Train up a child in the way he should go,
And when he is old he will not depart from it.

Remember that Kyle had a tattoo on his upper right arm that said, *Only God Can Judge Me*? Remember when we said that financial benefits would cease should a tattoo appear? Then Kyle put God's name in the tattoo…

A couple of years later on Thanksgiving morning, Matt was in the Dallas area visiting us for the holiday. I woke Matt up for the day—and saw a purple smudge on his arm under the covers. When he came out to the kitchen, I asked him about the shadow I noticed.

"Tattoo," he said.

"Yeah?"

"Yeah."

"What's it say?"

Mumble, mumble, mumble.

"Pardon?"

"Only God Can Judge Me," Matt replied.

I burst out laughing and caught Matt completely off guard!

"What's that about?" Matt asked.

I answered, "Well, I asked God to carve His name on your heart, but He carved it on your arm instead!"

Praise God!

Matt gets stronger and is seeing how blessed he is as more time goes by. It is such a joy to see him mature into a responsible, respectable young man. I pray God continues to bless Matt and bestow favor on him. I also pray that Matt wants to know God as his Lord and Savior.

Personal Reflection

- Do you have a child or family member who you are praying will come to know God?
- Do you have a prayer team lifting them up to the Lord in prayer?
- Do you believe that God can convince them of their need to know Him?
- Do you believe that He will, because you pray without ceasing for that precious person to come to know Him?

Chapter 16

ODD OR GOD

Psalm 37:4 (NIV)
Take delight in the Lord, and he will
give you the desires of your heart.

A couple of years later, I received a random email. The story was about a young girl who grew up in an atheist home. She began drawing when she was very young, around three or four years old.

She told her mom that God had taken her to heaven many times and shown her His world in visions:

His Son Jesus and His exquisite love;

Colors no human eye had seen;

Sights we cannot imagine.

Her name is Akiane Kramarik, and her paintings were beautiful.

I scrolled through painting after painting.

Scenery,

Colors,

Incredibly beautiful faces,

Jesus,

Angels.

I scrolled through to the last painting. It was a self-portrait of her at around twelve or fourteen years old.

This young girl was clad in:

White light

Ethereal, heavenly garb

(How do you describe heavenly things?)

Oh, by the way, the background—shades of rich chocolate brown (with gold, copper, and brass highlights).

Do you recall reading these words? These *exact* words? Minus the highlights. Exactly!

Two years earlier,

in a dream.

God gave me that precious dream of Kyle in His holy presence.

My husband says that coincidence is when God keeps a low profile. I love that saying!

Do you believe in coincidence? How could I have just randomly received this email? Showing her clad in the exact same heavenly clothing, against a rich brown background, as my son was shown to me.

In a dream.

Two years earlier.

Is this odd?

Or God?

Is He revealing another layer of conviction regarding His immense, holy, all-powerful, all-knowing, ever-present, loving Self?

I wanted to confirm some of these details, so I went to Akiane Kramarik's website to see more of her beautiful pictures. The one I thought was a self-portrait is actually one of a young guardian angel titled "The Angel." Here is how Akiane describes this painting:

> Sometimes we meet certain angels that appear like humans, and we don't know it. Many of us have been saved from many accidents, and we don't know it either. We should appreciate each safe moment.
>
> In this painting I blended a few dimensions to portray the guardian angels' mission: with the wings invisible to human eyes, yet with the see-through energy veil, the youthful angel is catching a falling child without any tension, difficulty, or worry. Her hands are relaxed. The background is gold, copper, and brass, to signify the providence, the law, and the safety. To save our bodies is easy for an angel, but what is hard is that sometimes she must allow someone to fall or get hurt, according to God's laws. And I don't remember why... (http://www.akiane.com/store/).

What is hard is that sometimes she must allow someone to fall or get hurt. And I don't remember why...

The exquisite beauty of her words comforts me, even though it has been six years since we "lost" Kyle. We didn't

really lose him…because I know where he is. He's dancing…
with You, Jesus!

And the highlights in the painting? Finding Akiane's words
are now the highlight of this moment!

Layer
    Upon
        Layer
            You, Lord God
        Reveal
    Yourself
To me
I am loved
    In awe
        Overjoyed
            and
                Blessed.

Thank You, mighty God, Abba Father. I delight in You and
desire to know You more and more fully, day by day.

Personal Reflection

- Do you believe in coincidence?
- Have you ever randomly received an email that had an impact on you?
- Or some other communication that took your breath away?
- Is this odd? Or God?
- Is He revealing another layer of conviction regarding His immense, holy, all-powerful, all-knowing, ever-present, loving Self to you?
- What highlights of the moment do you see?

Chapter 17

THAT ONE'S RIGHT

John 19:5 (NIV)

*When Jesus came out wearing the crown of thorns and
the purple robe, Pilate said to them, "Here is the man!"*

Romans 16:25-27 (NIV)

*Now to him who is able to establish you in accordance with my
gospel, the message I proclaim about Jesus Christ, in keeping with
the revelation of the mystery hidden for long ages past, but now
revealed and made known through the prophetic writings by the*

command of the eternal God, so that all the Gentiles might come to the obedience that comes from faith—to the only wise God be glory forever through Jesus Christ! Amen.

As an avid reader, I love to pick up a book and consume it as quickly as possible. A couple of years after receiving that random email about Akiane's paintings, I picked up the book *Heaven Is for Real* by Todd Burpo. It is a beautiful story that unfolds in conversations between four-year-old Colton and his dad, in the months following Colton's time in the hospital in a coma—or, I should say—when they thought Colton was simply in a coma:

> Colton said, "He had purple on. His clothes were white, but it was purple from here to here." He did not know the word sash. "Jesus was the only one in heaven who had purple on, Dad. Did you know that?"
>
> And I'm thinking, *Yeah, but how do* you *know it?* (Burpo, p. 66).

Huh. Sound like anything else you've read so far?

When we came across a picture of Jesus, we'd ask Colton, "What about this one? Is that what Jesus looks like?" Invariably, Colton would peer for a moment at the picture and shake his tiny head. "No, the hair's not right," or "The clothes aren't right." This happened dozens of times over the next 3 years. Sonja and I had started asking, right off the bat, "So what's wrong with this one?" (Burpo, p. 145).

Until they were introduced to the paintings by child prodigy Akiane Kramarik.

...that second picture of Jesus, a startling realistic picture that Akiane painted when she was eight. The eyes were indeed striking—a clear, greenish-blue under bold, dark eyebrows—with half the face in shadow. Hair shorter...beard casual...

Well, I thought, *may as well see what he thinks of Akiane's attempt.*

"Take a look at this," I said, nodding toward the computer monitor. "What's wrong with this one?"

He turned to the screen and for a long moment said nothing.

"Colton?"

Utter silence.

I nudged him in the arm. "Colton?"

My seven-year-old turned to look at me and said, "Dad, that one's right."

It was the only painting of Jesus that ever stopped Colton in his tracks. (Burpo, p. 145).

And painted by Akiane Kramarik, the same artist who painted the white light, ethereal, heavenly garb on one of her subjects, which matched what Kyle was wearing when he was revealed to me in heaven, in God's presence, in a dream.

Another layer of conviction, Lord God Almighty.

Personal Reflection

ᕲ Have you had an experience where different pieces of a puzzle seen to unfold right before you?

ᕲ And then suddenly when there are enough pieces, they fit perfectly into place?

Chapter 18

WHO'S SHE HOLDING ON FOR?

Psalm 4:1, 6-8 (NIV)

Answer me when I call to you, O my righteous God. Give me relief from my distress; be merciful to me and hear my prayer. Many are asking, "Who can show us any good?" Let the light of your face shine upon us, O LORD. You have filled my heart with greater joy than when their grain and new wine abound. I will lie down and sleep in peace, for you alone, O LORD, make me dwell in safety.

In late February 2012, Wrenette called Holt to say, "I've got cancer."

We had paid off a significant amount of debt from our part-time Plan B income as AdvoCare Independent Distributors. When Holt's company reorganized, he chose to stay out of a corporate position. The freedom gained from being debt-free allowed him the choice of whether he would work for someone or for himself and how he would invest his TIME. He chose to focus on working our own AdvoCare business. What a blessing that turned out to be when his sister wanted and needed him by her side in her final days. He had gained the gift of time. And he was able to devote his TIME to her.

The beautiful thing about our AdvoCare direct sales business is that it created residual income. That means income continued to come in. Even when life happened and Holt was busy elsewhere for a little while. People continued to purchase products. How blessed! We had built a business that gave him both TIME and money.

Wrenette wanted to discontinue her cancer treatment and come from Shreveport to Dallas to spend her final days with us. We figured six months, or possibly a year. However long she needed us, we wanted her with us. And she wanted to be with her brother.

Bless her heart. She arrived, went to the Dallas Tennis Classic at the Four Seasons with us, using a cane to get around. This was followed shortly by the hospice nurse's initial assessment on a Friday, with Wrenette using her cane to walk around the house. When the hospice nurse arrived the following Monday, Wrenette was immobilized and bedridden.

The speed of her failing health created a whirlwind of pain for Wrenette, which was devastating for us to witness. It seems that when she decided to discontinue treatment, she also decided it was time to go—and the time came swiftly!

Wrenette's dear friends, John and Carol, came over from Shreveport to be with her, as well. Thank God that they did, as Wrenette had converted to Catholicism—and I did not even think about a priest or last rites. Why would I? We had the hospice chaplain with us, and Holt and I are not Catholic. Remember, they were a Methodist preacher's kids...

Wrenette had not spoken for about a day, and we had to move her frequently, as she was incapable of moving herself. The hospice nurse, precious Sheila Johnson, asked whom Wrenette had not spoken to; Wrenette was holding on, for someone or something. *Matthew!* We had been so busy with her that we had not even thought to call Matt or anyone else. Wrenette needed to hear that her nephew loved her—and to say goodbye.

"Well hello, Matthew," said Wrenette when we placed the phone to her ear so Matt could tell her he loved her and to say goodbye. Thank God he was able to make a call to us in Dallas while he was at work in Lafayette.

We all jumped a mile with surprise—pleasant surprise— because she had not spoken for about a day. Even though she spoke, she remained immobile. Ashy grey skin enveloped Wrenette; her skin had once been beautifully peachy and creamy. How incredible to witness someone on his or her deathbed.

About twenty minutes later, the priest arrived to read last rites for Wrenette. Catholic last rites are beautiful—simply beautiful. All of the saints, starting with Father Abraham, Isaac, and Jacob, through Moses, David, and Joseph, were named and called forward to welcome their dear sister into heaven. When the priest completed this sacred service, Wrenette's countenance altered—completely transformed.

A soft yellow glow emanated from her previously ashy gray face and suffused the entire room with warmth and light. Remember, she was incapable of moving herself. What happened next was awe-inspiring to witness. Wrenette pivoted straight up out of the hospital bed from her hips, with her arms completely outstretched to the heavens, as that soft radiance emanated from her and filled the room. We saw—and felt—the very presence of God in that holy, sacred, life-giving moment.

Personal Reflection

- Have you seen the light of God on one of your loved ones?
- Have you seen "dry bones" revive?
- Have you heard the saints called to line up at the gates of heaven, to welcome someone home?
- Have you been in God's very presence? Do you want to be?

Chapter 19

BIG DATE

John 11:25-26 (NIV)

Jesus said to her, "I am the resurrection and the life. He who believes in me will live, even though he dies; and whoever lives and believes in me will never die. Do you believe this?"

When we left the room for the nurse to assess Wrenette, the nurse told Wrenette that she would not pass that day. Wrenette frowned. Did I mention that that day was the fourth anniversary of Allen's service?

It took until the following day for the "labor pains" of death to complete their work (as the hospice nurse called it).

I brushed her gorgeous silver hair and told Wrenette that she had a big date later that day.

Seeing Jesus, the love of her eternal life.

Being reunited with Allen, the love of her natural life.

(Let's not get into religious debate here. It sounds beautiful. It feels right. And I do pray that we see the people we know on earth in heaven.)

Hugging Kyle in heaven.

I was actually jealous for a moment. Or two. At least I am being totally honest with you.

Wrenette passed away on March 29, 2012. Exactly four years to the day after Kyle died.

I asked God to pour His grace on me, as it felt like a very heavy load to carry. May I share how good God is and confirm that He does indeed answer the prayers of His people? You see, God gave me only one day of the year to mourn, instead of two.

Personal Reflection

- Have you ever felt that you were carrying a load that was just too heavy to bear?
- Did God show you how His presence and His Word would lighten that heavy burden? Did you let go and let God lift it from you?

Chapter 20

HOLD HIS HAND

Romans 12:2 (NIV)

Do not conform to the pattern of this world, but be transformed by the renewing of your mind. Then you will be able to test and approve what God's will is—his good, pleasing and perfect will.

Exodus 34:35 (NIV)

They saw that his face was radiant. Then Moses would put the veil back over his face until he went in to speak with the LORD.

Lord, may Your Word radiate in and through me, like Your light shone from Wrenette's face, and from Moses's face.

I felt You, God.

"Hold His hand," Momma said. "He's always present," and You squeezed my hand back as a teenager—You still do.

Your hand stroked my heart and filled me with the peace that passes understanding, upon hearing of my sister's suicide.

I heard You, God. Out loud, once.

"I've got her. She's mine," You said about Bette.

So many questions follow a suicide. Your Word is sent for a purpose and does not remain in a void. Your voice quieted all my anxieties and fears—and silenced any human words that spoke differently than how You spoke to me, to soothe me— every bit of me—my mind, my body, my soul, and my spirit, mighty God. To soothe me with Your truth. Thank You, thank You, thank You, Lord God Almighty.

I saw Your name carved on both of my sons' arms, God.

You showed up—in a tattoo. Twice. *Only God Can Judge Me*. God forbid the tattoo, I know. I celebrate Your name in my sons' lives, Lord.

I saw You, Jesus.

You showed Yourself to me—dancing with Kyle—and You told me, "This is to bring you great joy. I taught him how. I taught him how to dance."

Praise Your mighty name, Jesus!

I saw Your holy face, God.

You showed me Kyle in Your very presence after his death, in absolute adoration and supplication, stretching out as far as possible in front of Your holy face, Lord God.

Thank You, thank You, thank You, precious Father God.

I love You so very much. Thank You for reminding me how much You love me.

I saw Your radiant presence, God.

On Wrenette's deathbed, her face filled the entire room with a soft yellow glow. Your glory and presence were seen at that moment, God. The Catholic priest, the chaplain, the hospice nurse, John, Carol, Holt, Wrenette, and I were all in Your radiant presence, Lord.

I saw through Jesus to the Father.

You showed Kyle to me, O Lord.

Dancing with Jesus. First.

Then kneeling in a fetal position like a baby in Your presence, Father God, in absolute adulation and supplication. I rejoice!

It was almost five years before I heard You reveal that truth, Jesus…through Me to the Father.

Recently, You revealed the moment with Kyle in God's presence was when Kyle was on Your mercy seat.

Holy Father God, blessed is Your name.

How many mommas get to see their sons in Your holy presence, Lord?

You are so great, and so good to us, Loving Father.

God showed up in my life—in the moments of my deepest hurt and brokenness.

Personal Reflection

- ↪ Has God showed up in your life? When?
- ↪ Did His presence reinforce, restore, or initiate your faith in Him?
- ↪ How did God reveal Himself to you? Did you feel His touch, hear Him, or see Him?
- ↪ Was it a breathtaking moment that eclipses all other moments in your life? Or did it take many intimate moments?
- ↪ Are you restored? Renewed? Revived?
- ↪ Have you moved from grief to grace?
- ↪ Do you know that you *can be* restored, renewed, and revived?

Chapter 21

YOU SHOW UP

Psalm 40:1-5 (NIV)

I waited patiently for the LORD; he turned to me and heard my cry. He lifted me out of the slimy pit, out of the mud and mire; he set my feet on a rock and gave me a firm place to stand. He put a new song in my mouth, a hymn of praise to our God. Many will see and fear and put their trust in the LORD. Blessed is the man who makes the LORD his trust, who does not look to the proud, to those who turn aside to false gods. Many, O LORD my God, are the wonders you have done. The things you planned for us no one can recount to you; were I to speak and tell of them, they would be too many to declare.

Father God, I praise Your holy name forever, Lord God Almighty.

At my breaking point, You showed up, Lord.

At my weakest, You touched my heart, Lord.

You comforted me with Your peace, O Father.

When I needed Your grace, You literally lit up the room, Lord.

It's all about You, Lord.

You are always here. We simply must remember to look for You. "To see Me—seek Me," You say—in Your Word, our life, our experiences, our church, and our prayers.

You show up.

At big times,

In big ways,

With a big impact on my life, Lord. And on so many other lives. Your will be done…

Thank You, God.

Because You, Father, are BIGGER than anything I shall encounter on the earth.

I love You, God. I praise Your holy name. In Jesus' name. Amen.

Chapter 22

A BOY AND HIS DOG

2 Corinthians 1:3-7 (NIV)

Praise be to the God and Father of our Lord Jesus Christ, the Father of compassion and the God of all comfort, who comforts us in all our troubles, so that we can comfort those in any trouble with the comfort we ourselves have received from God. For just as the sufferings of Christ flow over into our lives, so also through Christ our comfort overflows. If we are distressed, it is for your comfort and salvation; if we are comforted, it is for your comfort, which produces in you patient endurance of the same sufferings we suffer.

And our hope for you is firm, because we know that just as you share in our sufferings, so also you share in our comfort.

Psalm 147:3 (NIV)
He heals the brokenhearted and binds up their wounds.

Harry Allen Whartenby
Died March 25, 2008. Memorial Service March 28, 2008.
Kyle Wilson Mead
Forever twenty.
Died March 29, 2008.
Wrenette Mead Whartenby
Died March 29, 2012.
Allen and Wrenette's ashes were mixed at her request, and are
buried in the plot at the foot of Kyle's place.
Oh, yeah.
Joanie's box is at Kyle's feet too.
We finally figured out where to bury her—when we had to
bury him.
A boy and his dog.
Through Jesus,
To the Father

On His mercy seat!
So, where's Kyle?
I will tell you:
Dancing with Jesus.
So where am I most mornings?
In the kitchen…
Doing a dance
with Jesus.
Imagine
that!

Psalm 30:11 (KJV)

Thou hast turned for me my mourning into dancing:
thou hast put off my sackcloth, and girded me with gladness…

Deuteronomy 4:35 (NIV)

You were shown these things so that you might know
that the Lord is God; besides him there is no other.

Personal Reflection

Would you like to join the dance too?
And dance with Jesus?
www.DanceWithJesus.com

About the Author

 Susan B. Mead is an Ordained Sr. Chaplain with the International Fellowship of Chaplains, Inc. Susan's calling is to share her unique encounters with God, Jesus, and the Holy Spirit experienced during the darkest hours of her life, in order to bring hope to the grieving. She believes that her love story with God is not meant for her alone but was meant to give hope to many—as it is only hope that can get a broken, bereaved person up out of bed and back to life.

Susan is married to the love of her life, Holt, and is the mom of two "boys": Matt, who lives in South Louisiana, and Kyle, who is in Heaven dancing with Jesus. Susan and Holt live in Coppell, Texas, with Kyle's two labs, Brooklyn and Samantha.

6/15.

CPSIA information can be obtained at www.ICGtesting.com
Printed in the USA
BVOW03s2109260415

397758BV00003B/69/P

9 781630 473075